The Lord's Supper

— leading to Worship

F A Hughes

Scripture Truth Publications

First published 1973 by Central Bible Hammond Trust, 50 Grays Inn Road, London, W.C.1.

Copyright © 1973 F. A. Hughes

Transferred to Digital printing 2021

Second (annotated) edition (re-typeset, incorporating corrections and additional references) © 2021 Scripture Truth Publications

ISBN: 978-0-901860-60-6 (paperback)

Additional references are enclosed in curly brackets {}

A publication of Scripture Truth

Published by Scripture Truth Publications
31-33 Glover Street, Crewe, Cheshire, CW1 3LD

Scripture Truth is an imprint of Central Bible Hammond Trust, a charitable trust

Typesetting by John Rice

Contents

THE LORD'S SUPPER

Foreword

This book has been written because of a burden shared by a few lovers of Christ about the importance, relevance, meaning and infinite privilege and joy of observing the Lord's Supper.

On the very eve of His betrayal, arrest and crucifixion the Lord Jesus gathered His disciples round Him, and after the Passover Supper He inaugurated this simple memorial of Himself. In the Bread and the Cup He signified that He was about to give Himself — His body and His blood — for us. Then He added, "This do in remembrance of Me", so challenging the hearts of all the redeemed to obey and respond to such supreme devotion and love. In this act we also "show forth the Lord's death until He come".

It is sad to record that the import and appeal of our Lord's institution appear largely to have been lost in the ritual and formality with which it has been surrounded in Christendom. False teaching has given many to take it as a means of grace for sinners, whereas the Lord's Supper is a simple memorial to believers of the One who died for them.

In a day when spiritual truths are being despised or neglected as never before it is necessary to remind all true-hearted Christians of the supreme virtue and recompense in remembering our Lord in obedience to His request. As the Lord Jesus manifests Himself in the breaking of bread we may experience the joy of heart-felt response to the One who gave all for us, and of true worship to the Father whom He came to declare.

Our study, therefore, draws attention to the following truths underlying this service —

1) The Lord's Supper is essentially an occasion for Worship. God's desire for His people's worship is illustrated in His call to Pharaoh of old — "Israel is My son, even My firstborn ... Let My son go that he may serve Me" (Exodus 4:22-23).

2) God Himself delivered His people from bondage, as He has delivered us, by the blood of the Lamb. So they were set free from sin, the world and Satan — all being typified by the Passover. This deliverance was a personal matter — "every man a lamb" (Exodus 12:3), and so it must be with us individually.

3) "Christ our Passover is sacrificed for us: Therefore let us keep the feast" (1 Corinthians 5:7-8). This feast is quite distinct from the Lord's Supper. In Luke 22 it was after celebrating the Passover that the Lord instituted the Supper for the disciples collectively, and all who would love Him thereafter, as confirmed to Paul. So the disciples "came together to break bread" (Acts 20:7).

4) The Lord's Supper is unique to Christianity. Israel was never set free to the extent of the believer in

Jesus — there had to be a constant remembrance of sin by sacrifices which could never make the comers perfect (Hebrews 10:1-4). But we come to the Lord's Supper not to remember our sins, but to remember the One who has died to give us complete deliverance from them. "This do", He says, "in remembrance of ME" — not exactly what He has done!

5) The Lord's Supper surely takes us back in ever grateful remembrance to Him as He lay in death for us. A memorial must relate to the past, and in the Supper we remember our beloved Lord in death — we show forth His *death*. As J. N. Darby wrote, "The Supper ... presents to us the death of Christ — a dead Christ — His body broken and His blood shed" ... we "do not speak of the remembrance of Christ living in heaven."[1]

6) But this precious contemplation of Christ in all His supreme devotion and love unto death for His own is surely the spring of all worship. It is by His death that the Corn of Wheat has brought forth much fruit, so that in His resurrection the Lord rejoices in those who are now His brethren — able to know, appreciate and respond to Him in praise and worship.

7) The Lord's Supper itself, therefore, is not the end or climax of the service, but the beginning of worship. Israel's approach to God was not complete until the High Priest went into the Holy of Holies once a year, and then how remote for the worshipper!

But our approach to God is vastly different, for as we remember our Lord in His death we are led to

---

[1] {J. N. Darby, *Letters*, Volume 2, letter 9}

worship in a new relationship. No longer are we only forgiven sinners but the brethren of Christ, and "children of God by faith in Christ Jesus".

8) God had said of Israel, "Let My son go that he may serve Me" {Exodus 4:23}. It is remarkable that it remained for the Son Himself to initiate true worship to God.

It was consequent upon His deepest sufferings and abandonment as foretold in the prophetic word, that the Lord Jesus says, "I will declare Thy name unto My brethren; in the midst of the assembly will I praise Thee" (Psalm 22:22).

Therefore worship is most appropriate after the Supper, when we contemplate the risen Christ, now beyond death for ever, uniting our hearts to His own in worship by one Spirit to the Father.

9) The detailed instruction given to Israel of old indicates that there is a clear progression in the way in which God would be approached. The individual must first appropriate the Saviour personally. Then we are called together to worship collectively, and the Lord's Supper is a unique occasion provided for the united response of the assembly (or church), whom the Lord now delights to lead in worship to His God and Father. Little wonder that many find this experience to be their greatest joy on earth.

May the saints of God be liberated from all that would hinder their responding to this appeal of our loving Lord and Saviour, and may they learn to observe and increasingly value the remembrance of the Lord Jesus in the simple way He requested.

It has been truly said that "worship is the missing jewel of the evangelical church"[2]. This is the purpose for which God has created us, and only after we have become worshippers are we suitably qualified to be workers. Worship is the mainspring of true service, and the Lord's Supper is the supreme occasion for our worship of the One who calls us also to be His witnesses.

K.P.F.[3]

---

[2] {A. W. Tozer (1897-1963), *The Knowledge of the Holy*, 1961}

[3] {Kenneth Petter Frampton (1911-1988)}

THE LORD'S SUPPER

Part 1 —
A Personal
Memorial of our Lord

Chapter 1
The observance of the Lord's Supper

The Lord's Supper, being a great privilege, carries with it a great responsibility, both of which are conveyed in those challenging words of 1 Corinthians 10:16 —

> "The cup of blessing which we bless, is it not the communion of the blood of Christ? The bread which we break, is it not the communion of the body of Christ?"

In approaching this precious subject it is well to look carefully into the character of this Epistle to the Corinthians. It is addressed to "the church of God *which is at Corinth*". When writing to the saints at Thessalonica Paul in both letters refers to "the church of the Thessalonians *which is in God the Father and in the Lord Jesus Christ*", thus indicating the position of wondrous *privilege* in which these young converts were placed in their relation to divine Persons; whereas the Corinthians are seen to be in a locality where they are *responsible* to maintain a testimony to the truths of Christianity. Thus while the Lord's Supper is an occasion of immense privilege, unique in itself, we have to recognise the context of responsibility. This point will be the subject of further reference.

The Epistle is written not to the Corinthians only, but to *"all* that in *every* place call upon the name of Jesus Christ our Lord, both theirs and ours."* (Notice the very early reference to the Lordship of Christ, the import of which we may see later.) "All in every place" would preclude the assumption of "proprietary rights" or sectarianism, indeed the whole letter, its doctrine, its encouragement, its rebukes, its principles throughout, is the standard of divine truth for every true believer in Christ, while it is also manifest that the proof of spirituality is the readiness to recognise and own that the truth contained in the Epistle is "the commandments of the Lord" (chapter 14:37).

Not only had the Saviour committed this memorial to His disciples, but Paul had "received of the Lord" in glory the very words He had used at the Last Supper, and on this occasion He addresses every believer with that twice repeated loving appeal — "Do this in remembrance of Me" (1 Corinthians 11:24 and 25).

The early Christians evidently observed the Lord's Supper as their main service of worship. Although in this twentieth century the church has largely lost her first love for Christ, the Spirit of God would kindle in the hearts of all who love Him a desire to obey this appeal in all sincerity.

The mode in which this service should be held is not prescribed except that it was evidently observed with much simplicity. There was a complete absence of the traditional ritualism and formality which have since been introduced in Christendom, where many regard it as a sacrament by which blessings are conferred. But the spiritual value and intent of divine truths are lost whenever human ideas are introduced. Hence we need to cling to the simple appeal of our blessed Lord, who looks for the response of true and grateful hearts in remembrance of Himself.

Whether this is observed by many or by few (even breaking bread like the early Christians in houses) the Supper provides a unique occasion for worship.

There is no mention in the Epistle of elders or appointed officials, hence the practice of an *official celebrant,* prominent in the sphere of Christendom, is contrary to the truth of God as presented here. However the moral state of the company — and of individuals — is ever in view.

Likewise, expressions such as "dispensing the elements", "administering the sacraments", or "conducting the communion" are foreign to Scripture and tend to rob the sacred remembrance of our Lord at the Supper of its intimate spiritual value, since this is essentially a personal memorial of Himself by His own. In the New Testament the only priesthood taught, apart from that of Christ, is common to all believers, nor are there any distinctions drawn between what are termed the clergy and the laity in Christendom. (See 1 Corinthians 14:24-31.) All should be free to participate in the service of responsive praise and worship.

Our objective therefore is to enquire into the teaching of scripture on this simple 'feast of remembrance' as instituted by the Lord Jesus, and the great spiritual joy and blessing we may experience in response to Himself and to God, for "that great love wherewith He has loved us" {Ephesians 2:4}.

Chapter 2
Suitable moral conditions
— The Passover

*"Let us keep the feast ... with the
unleavened bread of sincerity and truth"*
(1 Corinthians 5:8).

In the earlier chapters of the Epistle Paul takes stock of these Corinthian believers. With faithfulness and affection (for they were his children in the faith) he notes their personal state, their relations one with another, their testimony before men, and above all else the measure in which they had, or had not responded to the truth of God.

Four times the Apostle speaks of them as "puffed up"; leaders held the place in their affections which Christ Himself should have occupied; their lack of grief as to the serious sin among them betokened an almost non-recognition of the Holy Spirit's presence. Partiality was rife among them; thus we do not wonder that when they came together it was "not for the better, but for the worse", and the atmosphere proper to the Lord's Supper was absent. With consummate skill, and in the power of the Spirit, Paul brings the truth to bear upon these conditions. He "determined not to know anything among them (you), save Jesus Christ and *Him* crucified" {2:2}, He preached among them "the word (logos) of the cross" ({1:18}, New Trans.), showing thus the mind of God in His complete setting aside of the first man — the man after the flesh.

In addition to the above failures, before introducing the great subject of the Lord's Supper, Paul recounts three matters which call for the most serious attention of believers if the Supper is to have its rightful place with them in practice —

(1) Sin must be renounced, and typically the feast of unleavened bread kept in self-judgment and humility (chapter 5).

(2) Idolatry, and everything inconsistent with the truth of our Lord's death, must be excluded (chapter 10).

(3) The recognition of God's ordering, in relation to Christ and human relationships (chapter 11).

The first of these — *the passover and the feast of unleavened bread* — is dealt with clearly and powerfully in Chapter 5. The *overt* sin of an individual was, without question, a matter of the gravest moment, but the *inward* state of the company, the lack of spiritual discernment of what was due to the Name of Christ, and the absence of sorrow over the dishonour brought to that precious Name, was perhaps even more serious still!

Pride of heart and of the exercise of gift, had blinded their eyes to that which the Paschal Lamb so preciously indicated. If they were to be spoken of by God as "sanctified" (chapter 1:2) then the death of Christ was a moral necessity. This was forgotten, and thus the man whom God had set aside in that death filled their vision — they were carnal! How precious and how challenging the remedy brought forward by the Apostle — appropriating the truth of the unleavened bread, constantly feeding upon it to the exclusion of self, and the formation of spiritual stature and discernment!

Secondly, the peculiar preciousness and challenge of the truth relative to the *Lord's Table* needed to be rightly understood and valued by the Corinthian believers, and as the first verses of the Epistle would indicate, by ourselves as amongst those who "in every place call upon the Name of Jesus Christ our Lord". This matter is dealt with fully by the Apostle in Chapter 10, and it is essential that the distinction between the *Lord's Table* in Chapter 10, and the *Lord's Supper* in Chapter 11 should be preserved in the minds of the Lord's people. The expression "coming to the Lord's Table" is often heard, and whilst not wishing to make any offenders for a word, it is nevertheless right to point out that this is not exactly what the Scriptures convey.

The Lord's Table denotes the fellowship to which we have *been called* and of which all true Christians partake (literally: have fellowship) every day. Chapter 10 stresses the importance of *our responsibility* to walk in accordance with the principles of this calling. In Chapter 1:9 the *faithfulness of God* as calling us into the fellowship is in view, and in this Chapter His faithfulness is again referred to in His constant care and consideration for His people.

In the earlier part of the chapter God's earthly people are seen in relation to the privileges which they could enjoy *together* — They "did *all* eat the same spiritual meat; and did *all* drink the same spiritual drink: for they drank of that spiritual Rock that followed them: and that Rock was Christ" {10:3-4}. Typically their sustenance and refreshment was found in Christ, and they had His presence with them. Wondrously blessed, and yet we read, "But with many of them God was not well pleased" {10:5}. It has been rightly pointed out that the Holy Spirit in these verses is not using *Israel* as a figure, but *that which happened* to Israel — the ways of God with them. The solemnity of these happenings are types for us. If we are to please God then our walk and conduct, not only as gathered together, but in *all* our movements, our whole pathway each and every day of our lives, is to be in accord with the "table of the Lord".

There is the suggestion in this chapter that normally every saint of God should be breaking bread! Paul in writing to *all* (Chapter 1) could otherwise scarcely say "the bread which *we* break" — this is not a word to a special few, although few may be in the light and blessedness of it, but it is that which is normal to Christianity. Thus Chapter 10 gives to us the responsibility attached to the breaking of bread, whereas in Chapter 11 we have the actual privilege of so doing.

But a few further remarks on this important chapter are called for. Many things are envisaged as tending to draw believers away from the dignity of the fellowship, and if any are tempted to think themselves immune from their appeal the word is "Wherefore let him that thinketh he standeth take heed lest he fall" {10:12}. Happily the Apostle continues that whatever the temptation, the faithful God Himself will "make a way" for us. Blessed indeed to recognise our own weakness; more blessed still to know and experience the faithfulness of God. Thus only are believers preserved as pleasing to Him.

The Apostle proceeds to show the richness of the fellowship into which Christians have been brought — "The cup of blessing which we bless, is it not the communion of the blood of Christ? The bread which we break, is it not the communion of the body of Christ?" {10:16}.

Is there any fellowship in this world that offers its adherents privileges in any wise comparable with those with which believers in the Lord Jesus are in communion? How blessed the realm whose unending, untarnishable wealth is measured by the precious death of our Lord Jesus Christ — His precious blood shed, His holy body given? The love of God of which that precious blood so powerfully speaks, and the personal love of Christ who gave Himself for us, pervade the life of which through infinite grace believers now partake. As drinking into this blessedness we are enabled to walk in this world, day by day refusing all that is inconsistent with the fellowship of the table of the Lord, while kept in the enjoyment of divine love and grace.

The Holy Spirit of God, through the Apostle, stresses (in verse 21) the fact that there can be no compromise in this fellowship. Let us quote the verse in its solemn challenge. "Ye *cannot* drink the cup of the Lord, and the cup of devils; ye *cannot* be partakers of the Lord's table, and of the table of devils." It is a moral impossibility! The title 'Lord' implies 'dominical rights' — He *must* be supreme in the affections if we are to be true to the fellowship — and thus able to partake either of the Lord's Table or the Lord's Supper in a worthy manner.

Thirdly — in the earlier verses of Chapter 11 Paul insists upon the order of God in creation being recognised and accepted. Man has fallen, but fundamental principles

19

remain — man, as such, seen in right relationship with God; man and woman in their right place with each other and before the angels. However opposed or contested, this word from God through the Apostle was to be maintained as the conduct proper to the assemblies.

Simple, yet heart-searching acceptance of and obedience to the truth thus outlined would result in an atmosphere in which the precious ordinance of the Lord's Supper would yield joy to the heart of our absent Lord. A suitable response in the affections of the saints would also be produced which, in the Spirit's leading, would ascend in worship to the Lord Jesus and to God the Father.

Chapter 3
The Lord's Supper

"This do in remembrance of Me"
(Luke 22:19).

It would be conceded by every intelligent Christian that of all the occasions upon which believers meet together, the Lord's Supper is outstandingly the most precious. There are features related to it which human words cannot adequately express, indeed the atmosphere in which our beloved Lord introduced it is almost beyond description. Love in its perfection was there — perfect in its constancy and in its service, and yet in those whom He would thus serve were the features of betrayal, denial and forsaking. "And there was also a strife among them, which of them should be accounted the greatest" (Luke 22:24). Would not the serious consideration of these things emphasise the importance of that which we have dealt with in previous chapters?

Apart from the Person of Christ Himself nothing in Christianity has been so persistently attacked as the Lord's Supper. The reason for this is not difficult to see. We quote the words of one now with Christ — "In the

Lord's Supper the heart is brought back to a point ... in which Christ and His love are everything."[4] This envisages a moment of intense joy to the heart of Christ, while His own rejoice in His love and respond intelligently and affectionately to it. This is something which Satan would hinder in every way he could. From the enjoyment of this precious occasion, when the *heart* of the assembly is responding to the love which went into death, every spiritual service should flow, both to God in worship and to men in witness.

It is an *absent* Lord whom we *remember*. We *know* Him now as exalted in glory and we rejoice in His exaltation, but we call to mind in the Supper the time when, in wondrous love, He gave *Himself* for us. Not only did He give "all that He had" (Matthew 13:46); not only did He "give His life" (Mark 10:45); He gave *Himself*. Precious Saviour — He, to whom the earth and its fulness belong, gave Himself to secure us for His eternal joy and praise.

It is important to notice that little is said in Scripture as to the procedure of the occasion, and we do well to avoid introducing what might savour of human ordering or legislation. But sufficient *is* said for the enlightenment of the spiritual mind.

From Acts 20:7 we learn that it was "upon the first day of the week, when the disciples came together to break bread". There is a great deal to be learned from that verse, and here again we observe the import of the earlier chapters of Corinthians. The "first day" would doubtless indicate that the supper should have an outstanding place in our Christian pathway, stimulating our affections to move in loyalty to our absent Lord

---

[4] {J. N. Darby, *Synopsis of the Books of the Bible*, 1 Corinthians, Chapter 11}

throughout the whole of the week *following.* Then it was "disciples" who came together — suggesting those who had faithfully followed the Lord during the *preceding* week. They came "together to *break bread.*" Hymns and thanksgiving of necessity have their place — *but they are not the reason for which we come together* — we come to "break bread". How sorrowful then if our response to His desire is withheld until nearly the close of the meeting. As we gladly respond to our blessed Lord, and He makes himself known afresh to our hearts "in the breaking of bread" what precious substance would be formed in our quickened affections, welling forth in spontaneous praise and worship. (See Psalm 45:1 and 2.)

There is a beautiful additional word in Paul's reference to the supper — "as often" {1 Corinthians 11:26}. We can perhaps understand something of the blessed Lord's desires in the Upper Room when He asked His own to "remember Me". He was, as we have noticed, surrounded by those who failed to appreciate His wonderful love, whilst outside the hatred and malice of the Nation and its leaders was rising to its frightful apex. In *such* circumstances His heart yearned for those who would hold Him dear in their hearts. But *now,* in the glory, His pathway of shame and suffering over for ever, He *still* seeks the affectionate remembrance of His own — and the Spirit adds the words "as often". How sadly this word has been overlooked in Christendom!

While the supper thus takes our thoughts back to the moment of deepest woe for our precious Lord, it also has in view His "coming again" {John 14:3} — "that blessed hope, and *the glorious appearing*" {Titus 2:13} are before us. We rejoice in anticipating the day when He will be publicly owned as Lord in the scene where He is now rejected and unwanted. Thus the past and the future!

What of the present? We hold the ground for Him in loyal affection! A few of His own, kept true in relation to his precious ordinance, are the unshakeable evidence of His eventual public glory. As Saul, the king, witnessed the place which David, God's anointed, had in the affections of the people, he was displeased, and said, "What can he have more but the kingdom?" (1 Samuel 18:8). How right he was! We rejoice in the prospect of our Lord's public exaltation!

No Christian privilege can surpass the blessedness of the Lord's own presence, and as each occasion draws to its close our affections would anticipate His presence afresh — soon "on the cloud", or once more in the Supper. The prayer of every loyal heart would surely be that this precious privilege may be continued to us "until He come"; and as it is preserved in God's goodness to us, may we be preserved in our desire to continue "steadfastly in the apostles' doctrine and fellowship, and in breaking of bread, and in prayers" {Acts 2:42}.

Part 2 —
Approach to God in Type

Chapter 4
The Passover —
deliverance from Egypt

"This people have I formed for Myself;
they shall show forth My praise"
(Isaiah 43:21).

In previous chapters we have, in the main, looked at the Supper in its relation to ourselves. We have thought of our responsibility to keep the feast of unleavened bread; the necessity of a walk consistent with the principles of the fellowship, and the joy that is ours as thus approaching the occasion of the Supper — a precious moment when we can drink uniquely and deeply from the streams of divine love — the sacrificial character of which, as contemplated afresh, endears the blessed Lord to every heart. We have, however, but lightly touched upon the theme of *our response* to Him who is worthy of a full and sustained note of praise and worship from every redeemed heart.

From the earliest days of man's history God desired a response to Himself, and although this was individual (no company was yet in view) He appreciated every such movement. He found pleasure in Abel's offering; He was pleased with Enoch's desire for His company; the response of Abram to His call (as the God of Glory) and his path of obedience as he "walked before God" undoubtedly rejoiced His heart. Would He not find joy in revealing His mind to one who would lavish his substance upon Him? (Genesis 18). It is recorded of Isaac that "he builded an altar … and called upon the Name of the Lord" (Genesis 26:25); and of Jacob we read in Hebrews chapter 11{:21} that he "worshipped". Thus God found His own portion in the responses of these and other Old Testament worthies.

Exodus and succeeding books introduce an entirely fresh movement in the ways of God — He is securing *a people* among whom He might dwell, and from whom He would receive a response consistent with the way in which He makes Himself known to them. In this section of Scripture we find the most precious typical references to the glories of our Lord Jesus Christ, and in the light of the New Testament it is not difficult for us to see the great thought of God that hearts should be so filled with a sense of the greatness of Christ that they cannot but overflow in worship and praise to Him and to His God the Father. Underlying all the happenings of the early chapters in Exodus is the command of Jehovah — "Thus saith the LORD, … Let My son go, *that he may serve Me*" (Exodus 4:22-23).

It is at this juncture in God's ways that the "Passover" is introduced, an ordinance of the greatest possible importance in the relations of God with His people — the Children of Israel. The immediate chapters of Exodus, and indeed much of the Old Testament, stress the greatness of the place which the Passover held in the

27

mind of God Himself; and thus the important place He desired it should have in the hearts of His people.

Embodied in the truth of the Passover is the way in which God would deliver His people from a condition of bondage, bringing them in liberty to Himself, there to know the joy of His salvation and to respond to Him in a service of praise and worship suitable to His own desires and nature.

The central feature of the Passover is the lamb, surely a most precious type of our Lord Jesus; a theme running throughout the Old and New Testaments right on to the last chapters of the Revelation. In Exodus chapter 12 there are (among others) two outstandingly important truths connected with the Passover lamb. First, as slain its blood was placed "on the two side posts and on the upper door post of the houses" {verse 7} in which the Children of Israel dwelt.

This was the basis upon which God would deliver His people from the impending judgment and set them free that they might, in freedom, serve Him. "When *I* see the blood, I will pass over you" {verse 13} — *it was God's own valuation of that shed blood.* Obedience to God's command in taking and slaying the lamb involved the recognition on the part of the people that they themselves were under the judgment of God and could be delivered only by the sacrifice of a substitute. The importance of this, as related to our response to God in worship, will be evident as we proceed.

Secondly — the people were to feed on the lamb, "roast with fire" {verses 8-9}. This is a most solemn matter, for thus appropriating and assimilating the roast lamb involves being in accord with that which had secured their deliverance. This "feast" was to be for them "an ordinance for ever" {verse 14}, they were never to forget the severity involved in the sacrifice by which they were preserved from the judgment of a holy God.

The first few verses of Exodus 12 indicate a deepening and progressive appreciation of the value of the "lamb" — "*a* lamb" (verse 3); "*the* lamb" (verse 4); "*your* lamb" (verse 5). The contemplation of the lamb, while kept in the intimacy of the home, would increase during those four days from the tenth to the fourteenth.

There are many references to the Passover in the history of God's earthly people, sometimes it was forgotten, sometimes it was kept with joy and rejoicing. There is an outstanding reference in 2 Chronicles 35:3-6 which shows clearly that the feast cannot be rightly kept unless Christ has His true place in the affections of His own. Josiah the king "said unto the Levites … Put the holy ark in the house which Solomon … did build … prepare yourselves … so kill the passover". The ark in its true place, the people prepared and sanctified according to the word of God, produced an occasion of which it is written "there was no passover like to *that* kept in Israel from the days of Samuel the prophet" {verse 18}.

Do not these things contain the clearest, strongest voice to us in our day? In Luke 22:1, the passover and the feast of unleavened bread are brought together, and it is essential that their import has its true place in *our* affections if there is to be the response to divine love which divine Persons are seeking. Unless we are set free from the bondage of sin and its consequent judgment, and too, from the power of the world and Satan, there will be no praise or worship from our hearts to God. And as we listen to John the Baptist's testimony — "Behold the Lamb of God, which taketh away the sin of the world" {John 1:29} — our affections would be moved to appreciate something of the suffering involved in the sacrificial death of Christ — the *work* of the Cross by which we have been secured for the service of God.

And as we listen to John's further testimony "Behold the Lamb of God" {John 1:36} — the preciousness of that glorious *Person* would attract our hearts, calling from them the praise which anticipates the great response of heaven — "Worthy is the Lamb that was slain to receive power, and riches, and wisdom, and strength, and honour, and glory, and blessing" (Revelation 5:12).

The atmosphere at the Supper in the appreciation of these truths has been referred to in a previous chapter, but it is essential that they are held in relation to *our Lord Himself* if their power and joy is to be truly known and experienced. In the days of our Lord's pathway here the "feasts of the Lord" had become "the feasts of the Jews" — the ordinance was outwardly observed with no appreciation of the blessed Person who is their Substance, thus the voice of affectionate response to God was unheard. The apostle Paul seems to have something of this pressing upon his spirit when in writing to the Corinthians he calls attention to their putting what was their "own" before that which was due to the Lord (chapter 11{:20-22}).

May we ever approach the Supper with the preciousness and the challenge of these words in our hearts — "Christ our passover is (has been) sacrificed for us; Therefore let us keep the feast ... with the unleavened bread of sincerity and truth" {1 Corinthians 5:7-8}. If this is our exercise and desire during the week (keeping the feast seven days) there will be on the "first day" an outgoing of praise and worship to the heart of our beloved Lord, and through Him to our God and Father.

Chapter 5
The offerings for the Tabernacle

"Of Thine own have we given Thee"
(1 Chronicles 29:14).

We have already noticed that God's desire in liberating His people from the bondage of Egypt was that they might serve Him. In Exodus chapter 15 we see them safely through the Red Sea, their enemies destroyed and they themselves, as led by Moses, celebrating the salvation wrought for them by God. At the beginning of their song they strike an exalted note, "The Lord ... is my God, and I will prepare Him an habitation; my father's God, and I will exalt Him" (verse 2).

Later in the song they appear to anticipate the end God has in view — "Thou in Thy mercy hast led forth the people which Thou hast *redeemed*: Thou hast guided them in Thy strength *unto Thy holy habitation*" (verse 13). It is evident that they (as often too ourselves) gave expression to that which was beyond their experience and affections — truths which were not yet held in power in their hearts.

The blessed God had redeemed the people to Himself with the determined intention of finding His dwelling-place among them. Herein is one of the most wonderful expressions of the heart of God — the full import of which has been made known in this age — to have His people in the appreciation of the "redemption that is in Christ Jesus", consciously near to Himself, "joying in God", and responding to Him in praise and in worship. As we appreciate our blessings consequent upon the death of Jesus (the subject largely before us), there would be produced in us an energy of responsive love to our beloved Lord and through Him to our God and Father.

This is surely in the mind of God as He says to Moses in the beginning of Exodus 25, "Speak unto the children of Israel, that they bring Me an offering, of every man that giveth it willingly with his heart" (verse 2). This was the heave-offering — denoting the energy of heart response. Thus we have the setting in which the remarkable tabernacle system is introduced, the sphere in which God desired to dwell in the affections of His earthly people.

The features and atmosphere of God's dwelling-place must of necessity be in accord with the holiness of His nature, and would involve those among whom He dwells having common desires with Himself. Hence the materials brought by the people (in verses 3-7) for the construction of God's sanctuary all bespeak His own attributes and thoughts, and are rich in their typical references to the precious truths of the New Testament. A full and true approach to God necessitates an appreciation of what each separate offering typically suggests.

Let us consider in a little more detail some of the various offerings brought for the erection of the tabernacle. "And this is the offering which ye shall take of them; gold and silver, and brass" (verse 3). Without question the purity and value of gold would suggest in a special way that which is wholly Divine — God's righteousness and glory in particular. Silver, used for ransom, would speak of God known in redemption through grace, whilst brass tempered in the furnace, would perhaps indicate His judgment of evil.

The true value of these and other symbols is seen in the way in which God has been revealed in the present dispensation and as, by the activity of the Holy Spirit through the inspired Scriptures, He floods our affections with the glories of our Lord Jesus Christ — the answer to every Old Testament type. As we consider these "offerings" may we ever remember that some understanding of them by the Spirit of God is essential for *our* approach to the blessed God. If the dwelling-place of God among His people was to be established these materials had to be brought — *they were the ordering of God.* Similarly on our part, there can be no *true* approach to God, no *consciousness* of His presence, or *enjoyment* of communion with Him, unless there is an appreciation with us of His righteousness and glory, the redemptive love of Christ and the refusal of all that is inconsistent with His holy nature.

The various articles enumerated in the following verses all speak of the moral and official glories of our Lord, an appreciation of which would produce a spirit of worship in the hearts of those approaching God. The spotless, holy humanity of our precious Lord, His royal and imperial supremacy yet to be manifested, but known and enjoyed now by those who know and love Him, are truths which fill our hearts as we, in our day, bring a "heave-offering" to God.

Every detail given by God in regard of the tabernacle (or "tent of meeting") and its construction has an antitype of the greatest possible importance to believers of the present day. Bearing in mind that this contained God's dwelling place, which is now no less than the true church — "the habitation of God by the Spirit" {Ephesians 2:22, Geneva Bible} — the truths presented are many and challenging.

As one approached the tabernacle almost the first thing to be seen would be the "court of the tabernacle" (Exodus 27:9). This was composed of hangings of "fine twined linen", fastened to pillars of brass, standing in sockets of brass. This *external* view of the structure is of vital importance! Varied and precious are the contents *inside,* but it is equally necessary that what is evident *outside* should be in moral accord with what is enshrined within. As we enjoy the great blessings flowing from the death and victory of Christ should not our testimony in this world be of the purity and practical righteousness which the "fine twined linen" would suggest? Let us also ever remember that the basis upon which we stand — "the sockets of brass," are of the same material as the Altar itself. Our every privilege and blessing is consequent upon the precious death of Christ.

In the Court were the Brazen Altar and the Laver. The Altar would remind us that the will of God, now so fully revealed to us, could only be established on the basis of sacrifice. The acacia wood (or shittim wood) of which it was made speaks of the holy Manhood of Christ; its being overlaid with brass would signify His ability to endure every test and phase of suffering, including the judgment of a holy God against sin, in order that God's will might be fully secured and manifested. Primarily it is the Altar of burnt-offering — in which offering is seen the unswerving devotion of Christ to the will of God, and the securing of His eternal pleasure and joy by His obedience even to death.

In that same precious death the love of God to men is revealed in all its blessedness, the question of sins and sin dealt with to His complete satisfaction and in full accord with His holy nature and the right of His throne, and thus are we "accepted in the Beloved" {Ephesians 1:6}, and set free to respond to Him in perfect liberty and praise.

Every offering upon the Altar was to be "a male without blemish", setting forth in some way the preciousness and perfection of Christ, pointing on to the great Antitype of the Cross — the very centre of all God's ways, the removal of all that hindered our approach to Him in appreciation of His grace. The absolute triumph of His love has been effected, the results of which will be seen throughout the eternal day, in a realm where God will be all and in all, His redeemed people joying in Him, and their affections filled with praise and worship. What precious eternal results of Calvary's altar!

The Laver (for cleansing) requires an answer from us of moral purity — a disallowing of all that from which the death of Christ should separate us. There can be no true approach or response to God if we are allowing in our lives that which is inconsistent with His holy nature, and which at infinite cost He has judged at the cross of Christ.

The priests in their approach needed to wash their hands and feet — our actions and our movements must be clean. Judicially we have been cleansed through the precious blood of our Lord, but we need the constant exercise of clean hands and clean feet, the cleansing of "ourselves from all filthiness of the flesh and spirit, perfecting holiness in the fear of God" (2 Corinthians 7:1). If we think of the subject of the Lord's Supper, we may well remind ourselves of the word, "Let a man examine himself, and so let him eat of that bread, and drink of that cup" (1 Corinthians 11:28).

In this day of moral declension and uncleanness it is essential that we fully maintain the truth of the Altar and the Laver. Even in the profession of Christianity moral standards are being lowered all around. May our judgment, therefore, be in accord with that of the blessed God Himself, so plainly set forth in the death of Jesus. Thus shall we be in every sense free to respond to God in full accord with His own desire for His saints to be "holy and without blame before Him in love" {Ephesians 1:4}.

Chapter 6
The Holy Place

"In His temple doth everyone speak of
His glory" (Psalm 29:9).

In the instructions given to Moses (Exodus 25) as to the construction of the tabernacle the first article to be made was the Ark, an indication surely that *all* was to take character from Christ, of whom the Ark is the most perfect type. This must be considered later in more detail.

In verse 8 of chapter 25, God had the whole system in view — His dwelling-place among His people; but for the moment we are considering *our* approach to this precious relationship. We have thought of the Court, with its Brazen Altar and its Laver and the importance of the truths conveyed by them in our movements towards the dwelling-place of our God.

Let us briefly consider the typical teaching of the Holy Place, in which were seen the Table of Shewbread, the Golden Candlestick and the Golden Altar. This Sanctuary contained only these three furnishings, and each one of them was of gold. The appearance therefore would have been striking, in that the light of the Candlestick (or Lamps), reflecting only upon this array of gold would have given a deep impression of divine glory — all teaching us of the resplendent glory of Christ. As the Psalmist records "In His temple doth everyone (or everything) speak of His glory" (Psalm 29:9).

The Table of Shewbread, with the loaves and their frankincense upon it, presents a delightful suggestion of the ability of Christ to maintain the saints in dignity and beauty (a beauty placed upon them) before God for His own pleasure. That the Table itself represents Christ personally is surely indicated in the "shittim wood" (His humanity) which was "overlaid with pure gold" (His deity).

The shewbread according to Leviticus 24 was to be the food of the priests, but these twelve loaves surely suggest the features of Christ reproduced in His people. Therefore there is something very precious in that the shewbread was to be before God continually (verse 30) — this was to be no transient state. The loaves were to be of fine flour with frankincense upon them — a continuous reminder to the blessed God of His own work seen in the moral features of Christ reproduced in His people! With what infinite joy our precious Lord thus continually holds His saints before His God — His purity, His beauty, found in absolute perfection in Himself, now seen, through infinite grace, in His own!

> Perfect in comeliness
> Before Thy face,
> Th' eternal witness, all,
> Of Thine own grace.[5]

---

[5] {J. N. Darby (1800-82)}

The loaves were to be set "in rows" before Jehovah on the table. This order must surely be *according to God,* whose order cannot be surpassed — no arrangement of man's invention could be suitable to the presence of God. In matchless grace He has brought us, in association with His beloved Son, into His presence for His own joy and delight, and as appreciating His movements of holy love our hearts must surely respond in praise and worship.

The Golden Candlestick (or Lampstand) appears to be linked closely with the Table of Shewbread. The detail given in relation to it is of deepest importance, and in general it suggests a ministry of the Holy Spirit — first lighting up the glory of Christ Himself, then maintaining the saints in the shining of that light, all in view of response to God. It is good to take account of the people of God from the divine viewpoint as sustained in the fragrance and beauty of Christ before God for His pleasure; it is also important to be maintained in the pure light of God's own mind as to Christ, and all that He will effect for His pleasure in Him. This is the normal function of the Holy Spirit of God; all ministry in the Spirit's power draws attention to the glories of Christ — *the light shines on the candlestick* — and as the preciousness of that glorious Person fills our hearts we are constrained by the Spirit to worship God.

The *seven* lamps suggest the completeness and perfection of the Holy Spirit's ministry, flooding the hearts of the saints with all the illumination needed both for a right approach to God, and for testimony to men. This light is always in accord with the *word* of God; there is no suggestion of "fresh light" — the *revelation is complete.* Certain features of the light may be *fresh to us,* but it is all in the Word, and we need to be preserved in constant fresh appreciation of the glory and greatness of Christ in whom every thought of God is centred and displayed.

All is to be in accord with the "pattern ... shewed in the mount" {Exodus 25:40}. God has been pleased to reveal His mind in our day in fullest measure, and all ministry and its resultant response to God must be in accordance with the revelation He has given.

The golden *Altar,* which also belongs to this Holy Place, has in its typical teaching a vital and precious bearing upon the subject now before us — our approach to God. We have spoken of the truths which are suggested in the Table of Shewbread and in the Candlestick, that is the place we have before God for the pleasure of His own heart, and of the light with which the ministry of the Holy Spirit illumines our path.

However, the golden Altar is typical of the priestly intercession of Christ as our Great High Priest — One who "ever liveth to make intercession" (Hebrews 7:25). The precious Saviour who "once suffered for sins, the Just for the unjust, that He might *bring us to God*" (1 Peter 3:18), now *lives* for us in the presence of God, maintaining by His service that faith and affection in His own which are consistent with a true approach to a holy God.

Chapter 7
The Holy of Holies —
God's Presence

"Having ... boldness to enter into the
Holiest by the blood of Jesus"
(Hebrews 10:19).

Unshod feet are needed in the fullest sense of the word as we approach, in our considerations, that holiest place in which the Ark of the Testimony was found. Let us at once remark that whilst we are engaged with the type, it is nevertheless the preciousness of Christ Himself which is to fill our hearts. How touchingly the hymn writer has expressed this most holy matter —

> 'Tis Jesus fills that holy place
> Where glory dwells, and Thy deep love
> In its own fulness (known through grace)
> Rests where He lives, in heaven above.[6]

The bearing and value of the type is appreciated and understood as the glory of the Anti-type engages our affections!

---

[6] {T. H. Reynolds (1830-1930)}

When the blessed God had the first creation in view, He commenced with material things and, all being to His satisfaction, He placed the man Adam therein as head. Happy communion between God and His creature in those congenial circumstances was apparently, alas, but shortlived.

In Exodus 25 *God starts with the Ark* — This was the first object to be made — the centre of the whole tabernacle system. In the Ark Moses, as instructed by God, placed the tables of the testimony (Exodus 40:20; Deuteronomy 10:5). How safe they were! Throughout all the failures and sorrows of God's earthly people the words of the Covenant-keeping God were securely enshrined in that Ark! The "manna" too was there together with "Aaron's rod that budded," but in 1 Kings 8:9 we read — "There was nothing in the Ark save the two tables of stone, which Moses put there at Horeb". The Ark was once more in "the most holy place"; it had been seen in varied places — Dagon's temple had witnessed its power; the house of Obed-Edom had known the blessing of Jehovah as the Ark had its place "with the family". Now David's desires were accomplished; he had refused to sleep or slumber until he found "out a place for the LORD, an habitation for the mighty God of Jacob" (Psalm 132:5).

Is it not delightful, beloved, to meditate upon the Antitype — the precious Christ of God! The incorruptible acacia wood of which the Ark was made typifies His holy impeccable Manhood; being overlaid "within and without with pure gold" sets forth the Divine glory of His every inward desire, and His every word and action.

The Ark was one of the smallest objects in the tabernacle system — but it enshrined that which was intrinsically precious to the heart of God. The One "meek and lowly in heart" of Matthew 11{:29} is in the greatness of His person beyond the knowledge of any but His Father. He who humbled Himself here was, and is now, the full and perfect expression of God's glory — "in Him all the fulness of the Godhead was pleased to dwell" (Colossians 1:19, New Trans.) and now at God's right hand "in Him dwells all the fulness of the Godhead bodily" (Colossians 2:9, New Trans.). With adoring hearts we read the Psalmist's words (confirmed by the Lord Himself in Hebrews 10) — "I delight to do Thy will, O My God, yea, Thy law is within My heart" (Psalm 40:8). The testimony is safe in the Ark! Every thought and desire of the blessed God will be fulfilled; every aspect of His glory will be eternally manifested; the transient communion of Eden despoiled by the failure of the first man shall be replaced by the uninterrupted communion of God with men in a scene of *eternal* bliss and joy — "the tabernacle of God is with men, and He will dwell with them" (Revelation 21:3).

Our hearts are bowed in worship as we contemplate the glories and perfection of the One who in holy Manhood (and yet He Himself "over all, God blessed for ever") could, in complete accord with the will of God, establish the foundations upon which the glory of God would be eternally secured and at the same time completely satisfy the heart of God expressed in His command to Moses "make Me a sanctuary; that I may dwell among them"; a dwelling-place not now confined to that which is material, nor limited to an earthly people, but universal and eternal in character and duration, a realm in which God is "all in all".

Are we not deeply affected as we think of the way our Lord took to accomplish that which should abide for the glory of God? In Gethsemane we hear His words "not as I will, but as Thou wilt". The Ark of old passed through the Jordan — typically the power of Satan in his opposition to the purpose of God was broken, the victory complete! Is it not significant that the Ark is there referred to as "the Ark of the LORD, the Lord of all the earth" (Joshua 3:13). The lowly Jesus, the Antitype of the Ark, is the mighty God against whom the powers of death and hell are impotent.

Hebrews chapter 9:6-8 indicates that access to the Holiest in the Mosaic economy was a very rare privilege indeed, but chapter 10:19-20 reveals the precious truth that in the favoured day in which we live, we have *"boldness* to enter the holiest", the Holy Spirit adding the solemnly important words "by the blood of Jesus". The immensity of the privilege is beyond all human thought. We are now free to approach the blessed God in the service of intelligent and affectionate worship, and that in the most holy sphere of His own glorious presence. At this point we must reiterate the importance of carefully meditating upon the whole of Hebrews chapters 9 and 10. The presence of God is *"most holy"* — the Christ of God, the "Holy and the True" fills that scene; entrance to that glorious realm involves moral accord with its holiness in those who would approach as worshippers. Thus every detail which the Scriptures unfold in relation to the Ark should command our attention and appreciation; if "Jesus fills that holy place" then, by the Spirit's power, that same blessed Person must have an abiding place in our affections too, and only thus shall we be free to enjoy the presence of God, our hearts filled with Christ and overflowing in worshipful response to God Himself.

The last three Psalms in the "Songs of degrees" are of the deepest interest. In Psalm 132 we see the exercise of David resulting in the Ark being found in its rightful place. In Psalm 133 this results in unity amongst the saints in the fragrance of the Anointing, and then in Psalm 134 there is response in the service of praise to God in His own dwelling place.

As we have thus considered the preciousness of Christ (typified in the Ark), may He have the place which is truly His in our hearts, drawing us into the bonds of holy fellowship with those to whom He is likewise precious, and thus may we together share in the present volume of praise and worship ascending to Him and through Him to God.

"And … the mercy seat". We could have no appreciation of the presence of God apart from the profound truth of the "mercy seat". In the type this was to be made of "pure gold" — it is the prerogative of *God* to "shew mercy". It was supported by the Ark — the right of God to shew mercy and yet maintain the holiness which is inherent in Him is based upon the foundation laid by Christ in His precious death. In the great day of atonement the blood was put upon the mercy seat *eastward*. Here is the basis for God to come out in the sovereignty of His grace, looking on to a day when, as a result of His movements in mercy, the whole scene will be filled with His glory.

If the way into the Holiest has now been made manifest then we can understand why the precious blood of Christ must have its place in Hebrews 9 and 10! Again our appreciation of the type is enhanced as we see the

Mercy seat now *personified in Christ Himself* — "Christ Jesus, *whom* God has set forth a mercy-seat, through faith in His blood, for the shewing forth of His righteousness" (Romans 3:24-25, New Trans.). How gloriously great this blessed Saviour is — sustaining every feature of God's will and glory — the One in whom God can move towards men in the sovereignty of mercy, "that He might make known the riches of His glory on the vessels of mercy, which He had afore prepared unto glory. Even us"! (Romans 9:23-24).

Four times in Psalm 136 the writer exclaims "O give thanks"[7] and in each of the twenty-six verses he gives the reason for that thankfulness — "for His mercy endureth for ever".

While thanking God for His abundant mercy to ourselves, shall we not join in Paul's exclamation of praise and worship as he contemplates the wonder of God's ways — "For of Him, and through Him, and to Him, are all things: to whom be glory for ever. Amen" (Romans 11:36).

"But as for me, I will come into Thy house in the multitude of Thy mercy: and in Thy fear will I worship toward Thy holy temple" (Psalm 5:7).

---

[7] {"unto the LORD" (verse 1); "unto the God of gods" (verse 2); "to the Lord of lords" (verse 3); "unto the God of heaven" (verse 26)}

47

THE LORD'S SUPPER

Part 3 —
The New and Living Way

Chapter 8
JESUS —
The Great Antitype

His Incarnation and Manhood

*"The Word became flesh and dwelt
among us, and we beheld His glory"*
(John 1:14).

The full value of a type is enshrined in its antitype! The importance of the Old Testament Scriptures lies in the fact that they speak of Christ! "The scriptures ... are they which testify of Me" is the tremendously significant statement of our Lord to the religious leaders of His day who failed to grasp the import of what they read (John chapter 5{:39}). They boasted in their knowledge of Moses' words, and were marked by pride and self-importance in their approach to God, but failed to appreciate that Moses wrote of Christ (John 5:46), and that there was no approach to God except by Him who is "the Way". They would not "receive to hold" (literally) the Word, the true Light that came into the world in the Person of Christ, but they did "receive to hold" the traditions of men. The Lord's word to them, "Search the Scriptures", was an appeal rather than command; He knew that those who truly searched would find Him to be the theme and substance of the Word. To those who, though momentarily disappointed and sad, had related the Scriptures to Him He expounded the "things concerning Himself" and caused their hearts to burn within them (Luke 24{:27, 32}).

Although an apparent digression the foregoing is absolutely essential if we are to appreciate rightly the subject of response to God in its New Testament setting. Every thought of God centres in Christ; He is the Yea and Amen of every promise, the precious fulfilment of every Old Testament type, the substance is in Him!

The New Testament commences, "The book of the generation of Jesus Christ, the Son of David, the Son of Abraham". Doubtless there are genealogical reasons for the order of the names, but there is moral significance also. The book records the movements in this world of One who would maintain the rights of God in sovereignty, and at the same time give effect to every promise of blessing to man. If man is to know and enjoy and respond to the blessings which God has in His heart for him, then the right of God to act according to His own will and desire must be established in the face of every opposing element. At last a blessed Man, competent to carry out every thought of God, is named — Jesus Christ! How essential this glorious Person is to God: how essential too to man!

Matthew's account of the Incarnation has Israel primarily in view, but the names mentioned in the first chapter have an important bearing on the subject of response to God. *Emmanuel* — God with us — indicates the deep desire of the heart of God that His creature man should know Him and respond to Him. A fuller implication of this Name is seen in Paul's first letter to Timothy (chapter 3:16), "God manifest in flesh", culminating in Man "received up into glory".

"Thou shalt call His name *Jesus*". This precious Name is on the first page of the New Testament, and it adorns the last page too. It is the preciousness of that Name which fills the hearts of His own today, forming substance which in the power of the Holy Spirit ascends to God in praise and worship.

"He shall be called a *Nazarene*." Various interpretations surround this verse, but the context shows its connection with Nazareth — a place despised (John 1:46) — His glory as Emmanuel and His perfection as Jesus and yet the "despised and rejected of men". True response to God involves that, on the one hand our hearts have a deep sense of the greatness and preciousness of Christ, and on the other hand a preparedness to move towards Him in our affections as the One rejected in this world (compare Hebrews 13{:12-13}).

The first recorded words of our Lord are found in Luke 2{:49} — "Wist ye not that I must be about My Father's business?" Paul in 2 Corinthians 1{:3} speaks of God as "the Father of mercies" (or "compassions" {New Trans.}). How often we read of Christ that "He had compassion" — truly He was making known the deep compassion of the heart of God. Does not this have a very important bearing on the subject of our response? "I beseech you therefore ... by the mercies (compassions) of God that ye present your bodies a living sacrifice, holy, acceptable unto God, which is your reasonable service" (Romans 12:1). The immensity of the blessing and favour of God, spoken of by Paul in the earlier chapters of Romans, if fully appreciated would produce this response of devoted service to Himself.

There as a remarkable verse in Mark 7. A man deaf and unable to speak aright was brought to Jesus who opened his ears and loosed his tongue. In astonishment the people say — "He does all things well; He makes both the deaf to hear, and the dumb to speak" {verse 37}. What a wonderful epitome of the work of Christ! He opens men's ears that they might hear the speaking of God, unloosing their tongues that they may respond in praise to Him. The verb is in the perfect tense — ears are still being opened to divine speaking and lips are opened in response.

Over seventy times in the Gospels we read "Verily, I say unto you"[8]. These are the words of the "Amen" — a name signifying "The God of Truth". It is remarkable that "Verily" and "Amen" are both the same word, and this has great import and significance. He who in His person is "the Truth" has brought that word of truth to bear upon men — teaching and drawing our thoughts and affections towards God — enabling us to respond to Him "in spirit and in truth". The revelation of God's heart, the wonder of His love, the making known of His desire, have been perfectly manifested in Christ and through Him the mighty response to God in a coming day will be commensurate with the revelation itself.

As we appreciate the revelation and out-shining of God towards us in Christ, may our hearts respond increasingly to Him in praise and adoration.

[8] {"Verily, verily" in John's gospel}

Love divine, our present portion,
    Heaven's choicest store,
Thee we worship, God and Father,
    Thee adore![9]

---

[9] {Inglis Fleming (1859-1955)}

Chapter 9
Jesus and His Brethren

His Death and Resurrection

> *"Christ hath once suffered for sins, the*
> *Just for the unjust, that He might bring*
> *us to God"* (1 Peter 3:18).

When our Lord was born into this world there was an immediate response to God on the part of the angelic host — "Glory to God in the highest, and on earth peace, good will toward men" (Luke 2:14). Emmanuel — God with us — was here "seen of angels". The full import of their mead of praise still awaits its manifestation. In the meantime He who will yet give effect in every detail to the angels' words has been "preached unto the nations", and in the sovereign mercy of God there has been a response even now to that proclamation — He has been "believed on in the world". Blessed indeed to be found among those who appreciate His preciousness and anticipate in their response the day of universal praise.

Should not our own affections be in full accord with those who in that day poured out their hearts' appreciation of God's Christ? "The shepherds returned, glorifying and praising God for all the things that they had heard and seen"; Simeon's heart overflowed as with the Babe in his arms he lifted up his voice in response to God — "Mine eyes have seen *Thy* salvation"; and the aged Anna "in that instant gave thanks likewise unto the Lord" — her heart responding *first* to God and then, filled with an appreciation of this glorious Christ, she must needs visit and speak of Him to *all*.

As we meditate upon this second chapter of Luke's Gospel, in which so many details of the birth of our Lord are given, we are solemnised by the fact that the same chapter so plainly shows this precious Saviour coming to die. There are four distinct references to this — a universal testimony to the sorrows of Calvary shadowing the glory of the Incarnation — circumcision (verse 21); "a sacrifice" (verse 24); the word to Mary "a sword shall pierce through thine own soul also" (verse 35); and the passover (verse 41). But this glorious Person could not be holden of death, and if the shadow of the Cross lay athwart the wonder of the Incarnation, the glory and victory of resurrection has dispelled the gloom of death and the grave.

In His life here below Jesus was "marked out Son of God in power ... by resurrection *of the dead*" (Romans 1:4, literally, {New Trans.}), and it is interesting to note the reaction on the part of those Jesus raised from the dead. The daughter of Jairus "walked"; the widow of Nain's son "spoke"; but Lazarus "was one of them that sat at the table with Him". Happy indeed the privilege we have of "walking in newness of life"; of proclaiming before men the virtues of our Lord; but more blessed still, in response to His love, to be found at rest and peace in His presence, ministering to Him in an atmosphere fragrant with affections from which the shadow of death has been lifted. John chapter 12 may not be the setting of the Lord's supper, but there is moral correspondence to that precious occasion to be seen in adoring hearts in which the Lord Jesus holds the supreme place.

Wonderful indeed were the movements of grace and power in the life of our Lord, but it is in His death and resurrection that the basis has been laid for God to be fully known and fully responded to. There is, among many others, one aspect of the death of Christ which is of peculiar importance in relation to our ability to approach God Himself — "For Christ also hath once suffered for sins, the Just for the unjust, *that He might bring us to God.*" There are depths of infinite blessedness in that verse! The desire of God to have His redeemed near to Himself, the love of Christ which would endure the sufferings of the Cross that those desires might be satisfied, and that those who were held in bondage through sin in distance from God might be set free to respond in the joy of nearness to Himself! The Church, formed by the Holy Spirit sent down from the ascended Christ, is a building against which the gates of Hades shall not prevail. The power of those gates was broken in the triumph and victory of resurrection!

King Hezekiah truly said "the grave cannot praise Thee, death cannot celebrate Thee ... the living, the living, he shall praise Thee as I do this day" (Isaiah 38:18-19). The inspired heading of Psalm 22 (Aijeleth Shahar — the hind of the morning) reveals that the blessed Saviour had the resurrection day in His heart ere He entered the awful darkness of abandonment. When this darkness had passed we hear the triumphant note, "I will declare

Thy Name unto My brethren; in the midst of the congregation will I praise Thee" (verse 22). The writer of the Hebrew epistle (chapter 2{:10-12}) takes up this same precious theme; many sons are being brought to glory, and in the meanwhile they have the happy privilege of ears and heart attuned to the voice of One who in the midst of His brethren praises God with singing (literally).

One of the most amazing incidents of the resurrection was the rending of the veil in twain from the top to the bottom. God no longer remained in the distance; in wondrous grace and in perfect righteousness He has *drawn near to men* in consequence of the death and resurrection of Christ. And we, redeemed by His precious blood, are free to *draw near to God* — the distance is not bridged, it has been entirely removed.

> 'Tis finished! loud triumphant cry,
> Ere Thou didst yield Thy breath!
> The veil was rent, and we draw nigh
> To God, through death.[10]

The tears of Mary Magdalene were stilled and her heart was thrilled as she heard the voice of the triumphant risen Christ. His mention of her name brought an immediate response from her heart — "Rabboni", "My teacher". Wonderful indeed the content of the teaching! Precious beyond all human thought that resurrection scene of victory and joy in which the heart of the Saviour was free to lead the affections of His own into a realm of unbroken intimacy with Himself in the presence of His Father and His God. *"Go to My brethren"!* — Can we measure the joy of His heart as He uttered those words! Those for whom He had given

---

[10] {H. D'Arcy Champney (1854-1942)}

Himself in incomparable love! — "and say unto them, I ascend unto My Father, and your Father; and to My God, and your God" (John 20:17).

> Now the Father's name Thou tellest,
> Joy is in Thy heart;
> In His love in which Thou dwellest
> We have part.[11]

Love has triumphed. Distance is removed and a realm of holy intimacy enjoyed in which affections are fully satisfied, divine love told out in all its strength and glory, and response secured from those who have heard and appreciated the message of victory — "He is not here, He is risen."

The Risen Lord has robbed death of its power. We who were held in its grip have been set free — free to move with unspeakable joy in a scene of intimacy and love where we can only worship at the revelation of divine love, expressed in all its fulness in our Lord Jesus Christ. We anticipate in our present response the universal tribute of praise to the enthroned Lamb (Revelation 5) and say from full hearts — "To Him who loves us, and has washed us from our sins in His blood, and made us a kingdom, priests to His God and Father: to Him be the glory and the might to the ages of ages, Amen" (Revelation 1{:5-6}, New Trans.).

For forty days the Risen Lord remained on the earth before His ascension to glory. During that period we hear nothing of the enemy's power — no adverse circumstance interrupted the movements of Christ as He manifested Himself to His own, filling their hearts with a peace which only He could bestow, and calling forth from them — in spite of their weakness and

---

[11] {Inglis Fleming (1859-1955)}

failures — a response which surely gladdened His heart. "It is the Lord", sprang from the lips of John; "My Lord and my God" — a tribute of praise which was unique from the heart of the erstwhile doubting Thomas.

> We praise Thee, Lord in strains of deepest joy,
> Responsive to Thy voice of holy love;
> We hail Thee, Source of bliss without alloy,
> Bright inlet to the light of heaven above.[12]

---

[12] {J. N. Darby (1800-82)}

Chapter 10
Jesus Glorified —
The Spirit given

HIS CHURCH FORMED AND SPIRIT-FILLED

> *"A holy temple in the Lord, in whom ye are builded together for a habitation of God through the Spirit"* (Ephesians 2:{21-}22).

In the first chapter of the Acts of the Apostles (more correctly called 'the Acts of the Holy Spirit'), there are four references to the Lord Jesus being "taken up" (verses 2, 9, 11 and 22), a universal testimony to the truth of the angelic word — "He is not here: for He is risen, as He said" (Matthew 28:6). From the very earliest moment the glorious truth of our Lord's ascension was attested by those who actually witnessed it; there remains no possibility of doubt! Mark records in his Gospel "that after the Lord had spoken unto them, He was received up into heaven, and sat on the right hand of God" {Mark 16:19}. Luke says that *"while He blessed them,* He was parted from them, and carried up into heaven" {Luke 24:51}. This was no apparition enshrouded in mystery; wonderful indeed was the event, yet it was seen and understood by His disciples, who as inspired by the Holy Spirit have recorded its precious details.

In particular we should notice with joy the twofold effect upon, and response from, those who were so greatly privileged to be witnesses of this wonderful event. Luke records that *"they worshipped* Him, and returned to Jerusalem with great joy: and were constantly in the temple, praising and blessing God" {Luke 24:52-53}. Mark says "they went forth, *and preached* everywhere, the Lord working with them, and confirming the word with signs following" {Mark 16:20}. A cloud had "received Him *out of their sight"* {Acts 1:9}, the dispensation of faith had begun, but the *reality* of His holy Person remained upon their spirits, they "worshipped Him", and they evangelised in His Name, conscious of His presence and support.

During the forty days between His resurrection and ascension the Lord had "presented Himself living" {Acts 1:3, New Trans.} to His own; had spoken to them of the things concerning the kingdom of God and had then instructed them to await the coming of the Holy Spirit, the power in which they should go out as His "witnesses ... unto the uttermost part of the earth" {Acts 1:8}. Christ Himself had been "received up in glory" {1 Timothy 3:16, New Trans.}, and from a glorified Christ the Holy Spirit came down to indwell those who were Christ's, fitting and empowering them to represent Him in the world from which He had been cast out. This was the commencement of an era distinct from every other dispensation. There was, and now is, a blessed glorified Man in heaven, and God the Holy Spirit is here in the saints.

Thus we have the unique character of the present day — Man in heaven; God on the earth. This is peculiar to Christianity. Stephen saw "the heavens opened, and the Son of Man standing on the right hand of God" (Acts 7:56). This was his testimony. He had, for the encouragement and solace of his own heart, seen "the glory of God and Jesus" — a living, blessed Man the centre of the glory of God. It is the attractiveness of that ascended Man in heaven, and the power and leading of the Holy Spirit resident in believers, that produce response in worship, and power and wisdom in testimony.

It is important to recall that Jesus had told Peter "upon this rock (Christ) I will build My *church* (assembly)" {Matthew 16:18}. For the great joy set before Him he had endured the cross, despising the shame — indeed how greatly He "loved the church, and gave Himself for it" {Ephesians 5:25}! Now as the exalted Christ He proceeds to build this church — drawing thousands to Himself by the powerful witness of the Holy Spirit.

Israel was being set aside as God's people, and now in the church both Jew and Gentile are being "builded together for an habitation of God through the Spirit" {Ephesians 2:22}. Christ Himself is the glorious Head of this church, and through Him we have the great privilege of access by One Spirit to the Father. God's earthly people, 'formed for His praise' {Isaiah 43:21}, had sorely failed, but now He has secured an eternal unfailing response from our hearts, because it is led and sustained by our blessed Lord Himself.

We are now considering the small yet mighty beginnings of this church, of which we form a vital part. But it is immensely important that we should realise the presence and work of the Holy Spirit now as then, so that we too may be ready to be filled with the Spirit for God's will and pleasure. Our understanding of the truth, the power we need for the practical expression of the truth, and for effective fervent prayer, the possibility of the precious features of Christ Himself being reproduced in our lives, the liberty of sonship, the appreciation of our glorified Head in heaven, and our ability to respond intelligently and affectionately to God in praise and worship, with many other things, are all dependent upon the presence of the Holy Spirit, and our obedient recognition of this.

Before His crucifixion our Lord had much to say to His disciples concerning the Holy Spirit; a careful reading of John 14, 15 and 16 would give us a deep impression of the importance and value our Lord Himself attached to the dwelling of the Holy Spirit among His own consequent upon His own glorification at God's right hand. In John 16 He speaks, among many other things, of three precious services of the One he refers to as "another Comforter" {John 14:16}.

First, "He will guide you into *all truth*" ({John 16} verse 13). The Lord had already said in chapter 14:26, "He shall teach you all things", and again in 1 John 2:20 we see that even the "little children" in the family of God have this priceless possession — "an unction (anointing) from the Holy One". In these days of departure from the truth, indeed when the truth is the subject of open attack, how blessed and vital is the presence of the indwelling Spirit of God — He who is named in both John's gospel and epistle as "the Spirit of truth" {John 14:17, 15:26, 16:13; 1 John 4:6}. Yet there are further important features in regard of the truth — we are to walk in the truth, to value and love the truth, our affections are to be preserved as girded by the truth, and we are to contend for the truth; but in addition to all these very important considerations we are to "worship the Father in spirit and truth" (John 4{:23, New Trans.}).

Secondly, the Lord indicated to His own what is perhaps the most precious service of the Holy Spirit "He shall glorify Me" (John 16:14). The context in which these words are found is overwhelming in its content. It is beyond our present scope to enlarge upon the greatness and glory and charm and power of the glorified Christ, nor can we compass the full blessedness of His following words — "for He shall receive of Mine, and shall shew it unto you." Who shall measure the "unsearchable riches of the Christ" {Ephesians 3:8. New Trans.}, the One so loved of the Father that He hath "given *all things* to be in *His* hands" {John 3:35, New Trans.}? How great are the glories of His *Names* — the Saviour, the Lord, the Christ, the Same, and perhaps sweetest of all — Jesus! How immeasurably blessed the glories of every office He fills — the Head (of His church and of all things); the Foundation; the Cornerstone (elect and precious to God and to the saints); the Advocate; the Great High Priest; the Sanctifier; the Upholder of all things; the Leader of our Salvation, of many sons to glory, and of our praise to God; the Mediator; our Surety (Hebrews 7:22) — a glory so rarely referred to! The list is far from complete — for He is infinite in His Holy Person and in His love and activities towards His own! With what delight the blessed Spirit of God unfolds these and many other precious glories of our beloved Lord!

Thirdly — "He will shew you things to come" {John 16:13}. We do not here enlarge upon this feature of the Spirit's service, except to say that by His inditing of the Scriptures we are left in no doubt regarding future events. Men may speculate, "men's hearts failing them for fear, and for looking after those things which are coming on the earth" (Luke 21:26). In the testimony of the Spirit of truth we know the glorious end in view, and that everything is in the safe hands of a glorified and victorious Man in heaven. By the same Spirit's testimony we know that the final events in this world will be viewed by the saints *as from above*. After the Church's history on this earth is closed the word is "Behold, a door opened in heaven, and ... I heard ... Come up here, and I will shew thee the things which must take place after these things" {Revelation 4:1, New Trans.}. The full and complete history of the Church from Pentecost to the Rapture, and all the subsequent happenings on the earth, have been recorded for the people of God by the Holy Spirit from heaven.

Much more could be said of the Person and presence of the Holy Spirit. By Him we are *sealed* — we belong indisputably to God. We are also *anointed* — the fragrance of *the* Anointed may thus in the Spirit's power be manifested in our lives; He, the Spirit, is the Earnest in our hearts, the assurance of our eternal inheritance in glory {2 Corinthians 1:21-22}.

A reference to Ephesians 4:30 may be salutary — "And grieve not the Holy Spirit of God, whereby ye are sealed unto the day of redemption." The Holy Spirit is sometimes referred to as the Third Person of the Trinity, but we must be careful to avoid any thought of inequality in the Godhead. The Holy Spirit is God — a blessed Person. We must not think of Him merely as an influence (great as His influence undoubtedly is) — one cannot grieve an influence! Although sent by the Father and by the Son He nevertheless also came in His own will. A well-known servant of Christ has said — "The Spirit comes from above, in His own power, to possess and fill the place prepared for Him" (J.N.D.[13]).

As we contemplate the wonderful blessings which are ours in this the Spirit's day, may we know more of the privilege of response to God Himself — "Because ye are sons, God has sent forth the Spirit of His Son into our hearts, crying, Abba, Father" {Galatians 4:6}. Truly such response is precious to the heart of God. The present habitation of God is in His saints by the Spirit; and we on our part respond in worship "by the Spirit of God" (Ephesians 2{:22}; Philippians 3{:3}).

---

[13] {J. N. Darby, *Synopsis of the Books of the Bible*, The Acts of the Apostles}

THE LORD'S SUPPER

Part 4 —
God's Presence
and
Eternal Rest

Chapter 11
Worshippers —
'Accepted in the Beloved'

"The true worshippers shall worship the
Father in spirit and in truth"
(John 4:23).

In the gospel of John, where the Lord as 'the Sent One' is intent upon revealing the glories of the Father — His Name, His Word, His love, His hand, His house — to the disciples, it is significant that the first time the Lord is mentioned as 'Teacher' (chapter 1) a realm of affection is in view. John's two disciples followed Jesus with the desire of their hearts finding expression in the words — "Rabbi (which, being interpreted, signifies Teacher), where abidest Thou?" {John 1:38, New Trans.}. "Come and see", was the Lord's gracious response, and "They came and saw where He dwelt, and abode with Him that day" {John 1:39}.

What precious unfoldings of divine love would they enjoy in the company of One whose dwelling-place was ever the bosom of the Father! The company of Jesus and the enjoyment of His precious love in sweet intimacy with Himself, would surely result (now as then) in affections suitable for fresh disclosures of the Father's love, in which He ever dwelt.

In two other instances where the Lord Jesus is seen as 'Teacher' the same atmosphere prevails. In chapter 13 "His hour was come that He should depart out of this world *unto the Father*" {verse 1} (this was ever the trend of His movements in John's gospel), and His faithful love to His own would so serve them that they might have part with Him. Again in chapter 20, Mary, from a heart filled with a yearning affection for her Lord, says to Him in Hebrew, "Rabboni, which means Teacher" ({verse 16,} New Trans.). Precious indeed is the way in which the blessed Lord would gather up those affections and direct them with His own movements *to the Father* — "I ascend unto my Father, and your Father; and to My God, and your God" {verse 17}. Had He not said at Sychar's well — 'the Father seeketh worshippers' {John 4:23}?

Drawing the two disciples into the warmth and embrace of love's abode, filling the Upper Room with the fragrance of His personal love, and making Himself known to Mary in accents of tenderest compassion as in resurrection He calls her name 'Mary' — He would thus ravish their hearts with the sweetness and preciousness of His own love to them and then lead their overflowing hearts in response to the Father Himself. This was His ultimate desire, but its full realisation awaited the presence and power of the Holy Spirit of God.

In previous chapters we have considered these and other movements of our Lord, culminating in His glorious resurrection and ascension to the Father's right hand. He has broken the power of death, that which held us in

71

moral distance from God — and as the ascended Lord He has sent the Holy Spirit to dwell with us in order that we might be enlightened as to His present desires for us. When here on earth He had said to His disciples — "I have yet many things to say unto you, but ye cannot bear them now. Howbeit when He, the Spirit of truth, is come, He will guide you into all truth: ... He shall glorify Me; for He shall receive of Mine, and shall shew it unto you. All things that *the Father hath* are Mine" (John 16:12-15).

Beloved, here are riches beyond all human ken! Who can truly set a value on the riches of the Eternal God! 'The riches of His goodness and forbearance and longsuffering' {Romans 2:4}; 'the riches of His glory' {9:23}; 'the depth of riches of His wisdom and His knowledge' {11:33}; 'the riches of His grace' {Ephesians 1:7}; 'the riches of the glory of His inheritance in the saints' {1:18}; 'the *exceeding* riches of His grace' {2:7}; 'the riches of the glory of the mystery' {Colossians 1:27}; 'the riches of the full assurance of understanding' {2:2}. Oh! the wealth, the untold wealth of the divine treasury! All centred in a glorified Christ and all made available to us in the service of the Holy Spirit of God.

The greatness and wonder of this immeasurable galaxy of divine wealth is borne in upon our spirits as we meditate upon the inspired epistles of the beloved apostles. We see therein the greatness of God's thoughts expressed to us in His beloved Son — *in Him* we are beyond death, raised, seated in the heavenlies in Christ Jesus, and above all accepted in the Beloved in God's very presence. Nor is this just abstract truth, but the love, light and glory of the Father's own realm fill our hearts and thus the Holy Spirit is free to lead us in worship to God Himself. How wonderfully blessed is our portion as the saints of God — emancipated on the one hand from that which would hinder our response to God, and enabled on the other to participate in the stream of holy worship which, led by Christ, ever ascends to the Father. "For *we* are the circumcision, who worship by the Spirit of God, and boast in Christ Jesus, and do not trust in flesh" {Philippians 3:3, New Trans.}. Happy privilege indeed — blessed to be in the practical gain and power and joy of it!

This service of praise may be enjoyed by us at all times, for by Christ we may "offer the sacrifice of praise to God continually" (Hebrews 13:15). But this privilege has been opened up to us through the precious death and rising again of our beloved Lord! How blessed then is the opportunity when together, having remembered Him in that death at the Lord's Supper, we contemplate all that has ensued for the praise and worship of our God and Father! We *remember* His dying and, knowing Him now in the glory, we share in His triumphs through infinite grace. Thus, quite distinct from our own blessings, the Spirit of God would lead us consciously into that realm of glory of which Christ is the Centre and Fulness.

This privilege of worship is most appropriate after the Supper when we contemplate the One who having descended into the depths for us, has ascended far above all heavens that He might fill all things. At such a time, with these glories before us, it is sad to find a growing tendency for ministry unsuited to the occasion, and which though good in its place, often disturbs or quenches the spirit of worship.

But as we are engaged pre-eminently with Christ, associated with Him as His brethren, and receiving fresh impressions of His glory and His love, He would lead us in spirit and in truth to His Father, before Whom our hearts must overflow in wonder, love and praise!

In this sacred realisation of God's presence, we may surely experience what the Psalmist describes as the "fulness of joy", and "pleasures for evermore" {Psalm 16:11} — our souls delighting in the One who is the Source of all blessing, as well known to us in the Beloved.

> Brought to know Thy Well-Belovèd,
>   Drawn to Him in boundless grace,
> Thy effulgence, love and glory
>   Shining in His blessèd face —
> We adore Thee, God and Father,
>   May Thy name exalted be!
> Praise and worship we would render
>   Now as in eternity.[14]

---

[14] {T. Willey (1847-1930)}

Chapter 12
The Lord's coming and appearance

"Ye do shew the Lord's death till He come" (1 Corinthians 11:26).

In a previous chapter a brief reference has been made to the fact that the partaking of the Lord's Supper has in view the coming again of our Lord. The importance of Paul's word to the Corinthian Church as recorded in 1 Corinthians 11:26, and of the grand truth contained therein, cannot be too greatly emphasised "… the Lord's death till He come." The contemplation of the first three words would fill our hearts, as we come together to break bread, with a fresh sense of the greatness of the One who has died for us — "the *Lord's* death", and of the extremity to which His love took Him on our behalf — "the Lord's *death*".

Glorious Lord, the majesty of whose Person is beyond human thought. Precious Saviour, whose love is likewise infinite and incomparable. One now with Christ has said — "Impossible to find two words, the bringing together of which has so important a meaning, 'the

Lord's death' — What love! What purpose! What efficacy! What results! The *Lord* gave Himself up for us — we celebrate *His* death" (J.N.D.[15]). As the reality of this great truth more deeply affected our hearts would not the Supper be marked by increasing freshness of response to our beloved Lord!

"... till He come." Precious as the occasion of the Lord's Supper is, the moment of its ceasing will arrive! The One we remember in His absence is coming again! The realization of this tremendous fact thrills the heart. Blessed indeed are the moments when He makes Himself "known in the breaking of bread" {Luke 24:35}; and surely His own heart is gratified as He receives responsive praise and worship from affections filled with an appreciation of His worth and of His wonderful love. Yet how much more blessed the thought of His coming again! With what infinite joy we shall hear His voice as He descends "from heaven with a shout, with the voice of the archangel, and with the trump of God" (1 Thessalonians 4:16). That voice will introduce an event of magnitude and wonder unique in the history of the universe — myriads of saints responding to the voice of the One whom they have learned to love, of Him who has been enshrined in the hearts of those redeemed to God by His precious blood. Those who are "asleep through Jesus" {4:14, New Trans.}, and those who "are alive" at that moment, will all be "caught up together" and will *"ever be with the Lord"* {4:17}. The path of responsibility and of privilege, even that of the Supper, will have ceased, but this happy portion of being "with the Lord" will know no limitation or ending.

[15] {J. N. Darby, *Synopsis of the Books of the Bible*, 1 Corinthians, Chapter 11}

How wonderful the atmosphere of the Lord's Supper is! Looking back to the cross with its revelation of divine love in all its matchless beauty; looking on to the future day of uninterrupted glory and joy; and in the meanwhile enjoying something of the incomparable charm and sweetness of the Lord's presence amongst His own —

> Thou dost make us taste the blessing,
> Soon to fill a world of bliss;
> And we bless Thy name confessing
> Thine own love our portion is.[16]

In Titus 2{:13-14} we read — "Looking for that blessed hope, and the glorious appearing of the great God and our Saviour Jesus Christ: who gave Himself for us, that He might redeem ... unto Himself a peculiar people, zealous of good works." This scripture shows the coming of our Lord in its two aspects, one event having two distinct results. The "blessed hope" is that which is the prospect of those who love Him and look for His return. The precious details of its fulfilling have already been referred to in the well-known verses of 1 Thessalonians 4{:16-17} — "The Lord Himself shall descend from heaven with a shout ... we shall be caught up ... to meet the Lord in the air: and so shall we ever be with the Lord." This will be the threshold of our entering into a scene of cloudless and eternal joy; a realm of satisfied affections! He will then fully "see of the travail of His soul, and shall be satisfied" (Isaiah 53:11). As sharers of His own joy, and in the enjoyment of His well-known love, we too shall know the blessedness of complete and full satisfaction of heart.

[16] {T. H. Reynolds (1830-1930)}

But beyond all else, the blessed God Himself will see the fruition of His own eternal purpose of love and glory, all secured through the work and in the Person of His beloved Son, and He, surrounded by myriads who will be like Christ, will share throughout eternity His own thoughts of His dear Son.

A further aspect of the Lord's coming is indicated by the words "the glorious appearing". This envisages the coming of our Lord *with* those whom He has previously raptured to Himself ("the blessed hope"), and has in view the inauguration of "the day of Christ" {Philippians 1:10, 2:16}, alternatively called "the day of the Lord" {1 Thessalonians 5:2; 2 Thessalonians 2:2, New Trans.; 2 Peter 3:10}. There are many scriptures which show the separate character of this stage in the coming of our Lord — "The Lord cometh *with* ten thousands of His saints" (Jude 14); "... the coming of our Lord Jesus Christ *with* all His saints" (1 Thessalonians 3:13); "When Christ, who is our life, shall appear, then shall ye also appear *with* Him in glory" (Colossians 3:4), are but a few.

In that wonderful day the erstwhile rejected and crucified Jesus will be supreme in the whole universe; His enemies will be made "the footstool of His feet" — that for which He has waited in patience at the right hand of God (compare Hebrews 1:13, and other scriptures). The effect of His exaltation will be twofold — every opposing element will be destroyed and He Himself will be publicly glorified and honoured; "the Lord alone shall be exalted in that day" is the repeated declaration of the prophet (Isaiah 2:11 and 17). But His exaltation will be the moment "when He shall come to be glorified in His saints, and to be admired in all them that believe" (2 Thessalonians 1:10). How precious is the result of the gospel testimony, for the apostle adds (in one of those important parentheses of Scripture) "because our testimony among you was believed". The movement of God in grace in the present time has *that day* in view. Paul could say, "He that has begun a good work in you will perform it until the day of Jesus Christ" (Philippians 1:6). He also had *that day* in mind, when desiring that the saints who had believed his gospel should be "holding forth the word of life; that I may rejoice in the day of Christ, that I have not run in vain, nor laboured in vain" (Philippians 2:16). Also he could refer to the Corinthian believers as his "rejoicing ... in the day of the Lord Jesus" (2 Corinthians 1:14).

While the unfolding of the truth regarding the *first* stage of our Lord's second coming is unique to the New Testament, both Old and New Testaments are replete with references to His later public manifestation, the day of His glory and power, a day eventuating in that wonderful moment which His present exaltation has in view — "That at the Name of Jesus, *every knee* should bow, of things in heaven, and things on earth, and things under the earth; And that *every tongue* should confess that Jesus Christ is Lord, to the glory of God the Father" (Philippians 2:10-11). How great the honour of serving the interests of Christ, as helped by the Holy Spirit, in *this* day, having *that* day in view, and knowing that everything done in faithfulness to Him *now*, will have His public approval *then*. How great too, the *responsibility* of so walking *now* that we "may be found blameless in the day of our Lord Jesus Christ" (1 Corinthians 1:8).

Our hearts thrill with joy as we meditate upon the richness and magnitude of the response to our beloved

Lord in that day — surely part of the joy set before Him when He went into death —

"Lift up your heads, O ye gates:
and be ye lift up, ye everlasting doors;
and the King of Glory shall come in.
Who is this King of glory?
The LORD strong and mighty, the LORD mighty in battle.
Lift up your heads, O ye gates;
Even lift them up, ye everlasting doors;
and the King of glory shall come in.
Who is this King of glory?
The LORD of hosts, He is the King of glory.
                              Selah." (Psalm 24:7-10).

"Sing praises unto our King; sing praises."
                              (Psalm 47:6).

As we await *that day* may we join in the doxology of John on Patmos, "To Him who loves us, and has washed us from our sins in His blood, and made us a kingdom, priests to our God and Father: to *Him* be the glory and the might to the ages of ages. Amen" (Revelation 1:5-6, New Trans.).

Chapter 13
The eternal day of God

"Behold, the tabernacle of God is with men, and He will dwell with them ..."
(Revelation 21:3).

We have previously referred to the unique character of the present period of time, the Lord Jesus exalted to the right hand of God, and the presence of the Holy Spirit of God indwelling believers on earth. It is a time of faith — faith which holds our affections centred upon a glorious object in heaven, as yet unseen but nevertheless known to us as real and living. "Jesus Christ, whom having not seen, ye love; in whom, though now ye see Him not, yet believing, ye rejoice with joy unspeakable and full of glory" (1 Peter 1:7-8). This is sometimes referred to as '*objective* truth'.

The presence of the Holy Spirit would justify the present time being known as 'the Spirit's day'. Since He came to indwell believers on the day of Pentecost His normal service has been to endear to them the ascended Christ ("unto you who believe He is precious" {1 Peter 2:7}), and then to form the features of the Lord Jesus in their lives and testimony. His formative work in us is referred to as 'subjective' truth'. Upon consideration it will be seen that these two aspects of the truth hang inseparably together, resulting in our affections being centred on Christ and His interests, and a consequent outflow of praise to the blessed God. We have already noticed that divine Persons are pleased to form and strengthen these features especially at the precious occasion of the Lord's Supper, when hearts are deeply affected by the unbounded love which took our Lord into death, and through death to victory and triumph; and from Whom, as ascended in glory, the Holy Spirit of God has been given.

In the preceding chapter the "day of Christ" was considered. This will be a period of great blessing, a time of joy and peace hitherto unknown in the history of the world. Christ will be exalted, His Name universally known — "they shall all know Me, from the least of them unto the greatest of them, saith the LORD" (Jeremiah 31:34). Satan will be bound, his influence removed; righteousness and equity will prevail (Isaiah 11:4); sickness will be unknown and death will be rare (Isaiah 33:24 and 65:20); nations will not war against each other (Isaiah 2:4); the brute creation will be at peace; "They shall not hurt nor destroy in all My holy mountain; for the earth shall be full of the knowledge of the LORD, as the waters cover the sea" (Isaiah 11:9). "His name shall endure for ever: His name shall be continued as long as the sun: and men shall be blessed in Him: all nations shall call Him blessed". The glad response from joyful hearts shall be "Blessed be His glorious name for ever: and let the whole earth be filled with His glory: Amen and Amen" (Psalm 72:17, 19).

> Kings shall fall down before Him,
>   And gold and incense bring;
> All nations shall adore Him,
>   His praise all people sing —
> Outstretched His wide dominion
>   O'er river, sea and shore,
> Far as the eagle's pinion,
>   Or dove's light wing can soar.[17]

The ministry of the apostles would, as assimilated by us, hold our affections in anticipation of this glorious day — "the day of Christ": His reign of one thousand years, which is also spoken of as "the world to come, *whereof we speak*" (Hebrews 2:5). This is a challenge to each of us! Is this day of Christ's exaltation the theme of our thoughts and conversation? Should it not be a *constant* joy to our hearts that He who was rejected here will then be the Centre and Object of universal adoration and praise? He who in His lowly pathway here was justified in spirit will then be publicly acclaimed as the rightful Heir of all things, and all the ways of the blessed God will be manifestly vindicated.

Glorious as this day of Christ will most assuredly be, there is yet to be revealed a day of more infinite charm and beauty, the glory of which is beyond the power of human expression. It is spoken of as the day of God (2 Peter 3:12), and is often referred to as 'the eternal state'. The world to come will be a complete testimony to the righteousness of *God's character and ways*, but the eternal state — the "day of God" — is a necessity for the *satisfying of His heart*. A heart of eternal love could not find its complete rest in any but eternal conditions.

Scripture has comparatively little to say of the eternal state itself. Paul refers to it in 1 Corinthians 15:24-28,

---

[17] {J. Montgomery (1771-1854)}

part of a most important and tremendously enlightening parenthesis in which he uses those attractive words — "that God may be all in all". Peter speaks of the same period in his second epistle chapter 3:12, where we have the expression "the day of God"; and John enlarges somewhat on this precious theme in the first verses of Revelation 21 — "Behold, the tabernacle of God is with men, and He will dwell with them, ... their God" (verse 3). Reference to "the end" in 1 Corinthians 15:24 most surely indicates *that* to be the great moment which God Himself ever had in view, and to which His eternal purpose, His counsel and His ways have ever pointed.

Everything created was to be for the pleasure of God (see Revelation 4:11), thus man as part of God's creation must eventually yield joy to His heart. It is important to see that it was God Himself who first sought the company of His creature — "the LORD GOD walking in the garden" {Genesis 3:8}. Alas! the sin of disobedience had resulted in distance and broken communion between God and man, indeed a state of enmity followed (compare Romans 5:10, etc.).

Succeeding dispensations have witnessed the patience and grace and abundant mercy and love of God — but the holiness of His nature demands that every contrary element must be righteously judged and removed if man is to be eternally happy in His presence, and capable of yielding joy to His heart. How completely the Spirit of God deals with the whole moral question in this grand chapter 1 Corinthians 15! The gospel — the good news of God — is introduced in verse 1, the preaching of which has brought into evidence the solid foundation upon which faith takes its stand, and through which salvation is known. Its threefold theme has cleared the ground to God's complete satisfaction. The death of Christ has dealt effectively with man's guilt; in His burial the man offensive to God has been set aside and removed; and Christ has come out in resurrection power, having ability to deal with every element contrary to God's holy nature, to reign in majesty and righteousness, to vindicate the ways of God before all creation, to "put down all rule and all authority and power", subduing "all enemies under His feet", and annulling for ever the power of death itself. Glorious Lord!

Then He, the Son, will hand over the kingdom to God that "God may be all in all". The great *end* has been reached — a realm of glory in which everything shall be in absolute accord with the mind and affections of the blessed God. Although as we have noticed, scripture is not profuse in its references to the eternal state, it has revealed in some detail the things which will *not* then obtain — "God shall wipe away all tears from their eyes; and there shall be no more death, neither sorrow, nor crying, neither shall there be any more pain; for the former things are passed away. And He that sat upon the throne said, Behold, I make *all things new*" (Revelation 21:4-5). Man's failures, ambitions and pretensions, creation's groans, Satan's malice and deceit, will have disappeared for ever. Righteousness, which *reigned* in the "day of Christ" will now *dwell* in absolute complacency in a scene where the nature and love of God will be supreme, and everything contrary completely eliminated for ever. The saints themselves will be *manifestly* marked by the very nature of God Himself — "the holy city" — and God will have reached the original desire of His eternal heart of love — "the tabernacle of God is *with men*" {verse 3}.

Every affection and desire will be completely satisfied. In the day of Christ the nations will rejoice in the blessings of God carried to them on the bosom of the "pure river of water of life clear as crystal", as it flows in all its fulness "out of the throne of God and of the Lamb". Fruitfulness and healing to a degree hitherto unknown will be there, and "there shall be no more curse". "The Throne of God and of the Lamb" will establish and maintain an atmosphere of righteousness and peace {Revelation 22:1, 3}. These happy conditions are measured by time, but in the day of God we reach the *fountain* of blessing itself; it is not now the "throne of God", but *"God Himself"* {Revelation 21:3}, and as freely drinking into "the fountain of the water of life" {verse 6} the desire of every heart will be fully and eternally met, and satisfied affections will find their joy in a never-ending theme of praise and worship to the blessed God — the Spring and Source of every lasting joy.

"Behold, I make all things new" (verse 5). No principle of evil shall ever intrude into that scene of eternal joy and unfading glory; Satan's power and man's failure will have no place there; death will be for ever abolished, and God will find *His* joy in the praises and the company of untold myriads who find *their* joy in conscious, uninterrupted nearness to Himself.

> Blest Father, infinite in grace,
>   Source of eternal joy;
> Thou lead'st our hearts to that blest place,
>   Where rest's without alloy.
>
> There will Thy love find perfect rest,
>   Where all around is bliss,
> Where all in Thee supremely blest,
>   Thy praise their service is.

> Eternal love their portion is,
>   Where love has found its rest;
> And, filled with Thee, the constant mind
>   Eternally is blest.[18]

As we await the age when all things will be reconciled to God may we rejoice in the portion that is ours *now* as "we also joy in God through our Lord Jesus Christ, by whom we have *now* received the reconciliation" (Romans 5:11, margin). In the enjoyment of this happy reality and in the anticipation of an eternity of unalloyed blessing, may we accept the challenge of Peter's word — "Seeing then that all these things shall be dissolved (present things), what manner of persons ought ye to be in all holy conversation and godliness, looking for and hasting unto (or hastening) the coming of the *day of God*" (2 Peter 3:11-12).

---

[18] {J. N. Darby (1800-82)}

Conclusion

The observance of the Lord's Supper is without question unique among the many privileges which are ours, as Christians, to enjoy. Happy indeed are the gatherings together for prayer, for the study of God's holy Word, for the ministry of that Word, and for the announcing of the precious Gospel; but each of these occasions would be enriched as the affections of believers were freshly kindled and strengthened by a deeper appreciation of the love of Christ — love which so blessedly attracts and fills the heart as we remember the One who "though He was rich, yet for your (our) sakes He became poor, that ye (we) through His poverty might be rich" {2 Corinthians 8:9}.

Each coming together should impress its own peculiar feature upon those gathered — the meeting for prayer should be marked by deep pulsation of concern for the interests of our Lord; that for the reading of God's Word should produce a desire for the mind to be enriched and formed by the truth itself; and in the witness of the Gospel a deep compassion that others might be brought to know the love of the Saviour. But in the Supper it is the *heart* of the assembly which is so deeply affected. It is *Himself* — and He alone who engages the affections — and from hearts thus attracted and affected surely a volume of praise and worship to Christ, and through Him to the Father, should flow forth spontaneously in the Spirit's power.

We are thankful that this most precious and holy occasion has been preserved to us, and that in its pristine beauty and simplicity. In a spirit of profound thankfulness to our God may we recognise more intelligently *His own* desires — that we should be a people, not only appreciating our own wonderful blessings, but rising to the greatness of our privilege in responding to His own great heart of love.

We have been brought, at infinite cost, to the very source of divine love. "For through Him (Christ) we both have access by One Spirit unto the Father" (Ephesians 2:18). The whole Godhead is in that verse. All the love and power and glory of Divine Persons is involved in our being brought into nearness — and into the present and eternal enjoyment of God's favour and presence. Should not our response be, in some measure at least, in accord with this wonderful outpouring of the heart of God?

Blessed indeed if that response is begun and increased here and now! Soon the day of eternity will witness the sustained note of praise and worship in a realm of fully satisfied desire and affection.

However, we cannot conclude this subject of the Lord's Supper without lamenting again the sad state of indifference and departure which has allowed this privilege, so graciously entrusted to us, to be widely surrendered in these last days. How many, alas, seem to have left their First Love, or no longer feel constrained to remember the One who died for them, as He appointed.

It is therefore our earnest prayer and appeal that all who read this book may be challenged by the Lord, and awakened in their affections towards Him. May we also help in true spiritual energy to encourage the revival of this precious observance of breaking bread wherever possible — even by the twos or threes, or "from house to house" — in obedience to our Lord's loving request to His own, and so to show forth His death until He comes.

F.A.H.